Christmas
in
Grandma's Day

Christmas in Grandma's Day

Faye Gardner
with Jennifer Collins

Evans

In Grandma's Day
Christmas In Grandma's Day
Having Fun In Grandma's Day
Home Life In Grandma's Day
School Life In Grandma's Day
Travelling In Grandma's Day

Published by Evans Brothers Ltd
2A Portman Mansions
Chiltern Street
London W1M 1LE
England

First published in 1997
Printed in Hong Kong

British Library Cataloguing in Publication Data
Gardner, Faye
Christmas in Grandma's day 1. Christmas – History – 20th century – Juvenile literature
I. Title
394.2'663'09045

ISBN 0 237 51830 9

Acknowledgements
Planning and production by The Creative Publishing Company
Edited by Faye Gardner
Designed by Ian Winton
Commissioned photography by R Hammonds
Illustrations by Jenny Mumford

The publishers would like to thank Barbara Pugh and Jennifer Collins for their kind help in the preparation of this book.

For permission to reproduce copyright material, the author
and publishers gratefully acknowledge the following:
Advertising Archive Ltd.: 31 (bottom), Aquarius Picture Library: 18 (bottom);
Barnaby's Picture Library: 19, 34 (bottom), 35 (bottom); Radio Times: 40; Beamish, The North of England
Open Air Museum, County Durham: 15 (bottom), 22 (top), 31 (top), 35 (top), 43; Bourne Hall Museum, Ewell: 8 (centre left);
Christmas Archives International: cover (front, bottom left), 30 (top); Hulton Getty: 10 (bottom), 11 (bottom), 14 (bottom),
22 (bottom), 24 (top), 38; Last Resort: 10 (top), 37 (top), 41 (top); London Metropolitan Archives: 13 (bottom); PA News: 18 (top);
Popperfoto: cover (front, top left); The Robert Opie Collection: cover (front right), 11 (top), 13 (top), 15 (top),
21 (bottom, centre right), 24 (bottom left, right), 25, 28 (centre, bottom), 36, 37 (centre, bottom), 39;
Topham Picturepoint: 20, 21 (top).

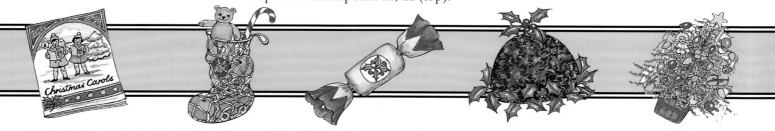

CONTENTS

My name is Jennifer. I am a grandmother. I have one grandchild, Bobby, who is ten years old.

I was born in 1938, one year before the start of the Second World War. I grew up in a town called Stoneleigh, which is very close to London. The photo below shows you how the town looked then.

This is the house I grew up in.

During the war my dad was a soldier in the army, so he spent a lot of time away from home. My mum was a housewife. I had an older brother called Peter to play with.

Christmas was my favourite time of year when I was little. Christmas and birthdays were the only times that we were given presents like toys and sweets.

I am going to tell you what Christmas was like when I was young and how things were different then.

9

Every November I started saving my pocket money to buy Christmas presents for my family. I was lucky because my grandad always gave me some money, too.

During the year he collected threepenny coins in an old jam jar. At Christmas time he shared some of the money between my brother and me. We got six threepenny coins each. That's one shilling and six old pence or 9p in today's money. That seemed a lot of money when I was little. I felt rich!

About a week before Christmas my mum took my brother and me to London to look around the shops. It was very exciting. The streets were crowded with shoppers and it was very noisy.

Some department stores had doormen dressed in Father Christmas costumes. They walked up and down the pavement ringing handbells and shouting, 'Merry Christmas!' to invite people into the store.

I loved to look at the toy displays in the windows. I had never seen so many dolls and teddy bears!

Inside the toy departments the floors were covered with electric train sets and there were tables piled with clockwork toys for us to play with. Clockwork toys had a little key which you wound up to make them move.

During wartime many streets had rows of sandbags piled up against the buildings to protect them against bombs. We used to stand on the sandbags to see inside the windows. Shops weren't allowed to light up their windows at night. Lights could help guide enemy bomber planes to their target.

Some of the toy departments had a Santa's grotto specially built at Christmas time for children visiting the store. The grotto was usually a little room painted to look like Santa's house. You paid to go inside and get a present from Santa Claus. I was too scared to go in by myself, so my brother came with me. Here he is with Santa.

One year Santa gave me a baby doll and Peter got a book of puzzles and tricks. These puzzles came from the book. Try them out on your friends.

Twenty-four match puzzle

The puzzle

1) Place twenty-four used matches as shown in the picture.
2) Ask your friend to take away eight matches so that two squares are left on the table.

The answer

This picture shows you which matches need to be removed to leave two complete squares.

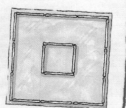

Walk through a Christmas card

The puzzle

1) Show your friend an old Christmas card (or a piece of paper about the same size).
2) Ask them if they can think of a way of cutting a hole in the card that would be big enough for a person to walk through.

The answer

1) Unfold the card and cut a slit along the fold, leaving a 0.5cm gap at the top and bottom of the fold.

2) Fold the card and cut thin strips alternately from the edges to the slit at the middle, and then from the slit nearly to the edges.

3) When you have finished, unfold the card into a zig-zag loop big enough to be passed over your body.

Crack-a-joke
What would you get if
you crossed Santa with a
flying saucer?
¡oH - ¡oH - ¡oH - ɟ-n∀

Another year Santa gave me a magic painting book. Instead of using paints to colour in the pictures you just painted each page with water and the pictures turned different colours by themselves.

After we'd looked around the shops my mum took us to a tearoom for icecream sundaes. The tearoom was in a building called the Lyons Corner House, which had a different restaurant on each floor. In the centre of the room there were two musicians who played a piano and double-bass to entertain the customers.

We were served by waitresses dressed in smart uniforms. I ordered a steamboat sundae, which was banana and icecream shaped to look like a boat. It had chocolate chips sprinkled on the top.

When I was seven I went to a Christmas party for children whose dads belonged to the **armed forces**. I wore my best dress and my mum curled my hair with metal tongs that had to be heated up on the gas cooker.

The party was held in a huge hall filled with rows of tables piled high with food. It was a real treat to have so much to eat! Most of the sandwiches were filled with different flavoured pastes. For pudding we ate fairy cakes, currant buns and sponge fingers spread with jam.

Christmas Carols

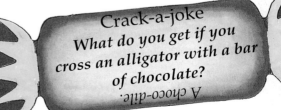

At one end of the hall there was a stage and a Christmas tree decorated with wrapped presents. After we'd finished eating, some of the older children got up on the stage and performed little acts to entertain us. One of the girls sang a song called *Alice Blue Gown*, a boy played the piano and another girl tap-danced to a Shirley Temple record.

Afterwards we played games like pass-the-parcel, musical bumps and musical statues. The winner of each game was given a present from the Christmas tree. I won a bar of chocolate. That was a big thrill for me because I'd never had a whole bar of chocolate before!

At the end of the party everyone was given a balloon to take home.

Crack-a-joke
What do you get if you cross an alligator with a bar of chocolate?

A choco-dile.

'Here are some of my favourite games.'

Here are some of my favourite party games that I played when I was young.

PIN SANTA'S BEARD

To play this game you need to have a big drawing of Santa Claus on a piece of card and a cardboard beard to stick on Santa's face. You can trace the beard shape on this page to make your own. Before you start the game you need to get ready a pile of small gifts on a table in the room. Stick a different number on each gift. Give everyone a piece of paper with their name on it. Each piece of paper is numbered the same as a gift in the pile. You also need to wrap an extra present for the winner.

How to play

1 Stick the picture of Santa Claus on one of the walls in the room with some Blu-tack.

2 Put a wrapped present (for the winner) beside the picture of Santa Claus.

3 Every child takes it in turns to be blindfolded.

4 The child wearing the blindfold is spun around three times on the spot. Then he or she has to try and stick the beard on the correct part of Santa's face. The piece of paper with the child's name on it is used to mark the spot where they stick the beard.

5 Whoever sticks the beard nearest to the correct place on Santa's face wins Santa Claus's present, as well as a gift from the pile. Everyone else gets a gift from the pile that is numbered the same as their piece of paper.

FRUIT BASKET

Before you start to play you need to make a circle out of chairs (one chair for each person playing the game). One person is the 'caller'; everyone else sits on a chair in the circle.

How to play

The caller divides the group into different kinds of fruit. For example, some children are apples, other children are bananas, peaches, plums or oranges.
The caller shouts out different orders to the group. For example, 'Apples swap with pears!' or 'Bananas swap with plums!'
The children who are apples have to change places with the children who are pears and so on. If the caller shouts 'Fruit basket!' everyone has to swap places with everyone else. As soon as everyone has swapped places, the caller quickly shouts out a new order.

If somebody stands up without being called, then they are 'out'. Whoever sits down last is also 'out'. The winner is the very last child to be caught out.

TOSS THE SPOON

How to play

Everyone sits on a chair in a circle. Each child chooses the name of an animal – horse, dog, cat, rabbit and so on. One of the children has a spoon. He or she throws it up in the air at the same time calling the name of one of the animals.

The child who has chosen that animal must catch the spoon before it touches the ground, toss it up again and call out another animal. If anyone, when called, lets the spoon touch the ground, then they are 'out'. The winner is the last person to be caught out.

17

After school my brother and I went carol singing with some friends who lived nearby. We borrowed my dad's oil lamp and went to other houses in our street. We sang songs like *We Wish You a Merry Christmas* and *Away in a Manger*. Sometimes we got as much as sixpence, which seemed a lot of money to me! I spent the money on Christmas presents. If I had any money left over I went to the cinema. I loved *The Wizard of Oz* and saw it three times!

Crack-a-joke
What do they sing in the desert at Christmas?

Oh camel ye faithful.

METRO • GOLDWYN • MAYER • PRESENTS

the WIZARD of OZ

A VICTOR FLEMING PRODUCTION PRODUCED BY MERVYN LeROY

in TECHNICOLOR

with
JUDY **GARLAND**
FRANK **MORGAN**
RAY **BOLGER**
BERT **LAHR**
JACK **HALEY**

BILLIE **BURKE** • MARGARET **HAMILTON** • CHARLEY **GRAPEWIN** • AND THE **MUNCHKINS**
SCREENPLAY BY NOEL LANGLEY, FLORENCE RYERSON AND EDGAR ALLAN WOOLF
BASED ON THE BOOK BY L. FRANK BAUM • DIRECTED BY VICTOR FLEMING

When I was eleven I joined a carol singing group which was organised by a school teacher called Mr Dymock, who lived in the same street as me. I felt very grown up because we were given song sheets and learned to sing one or two carols in **Latin**.

Rich people lived at some of the houses we visited. We were invited inside and given mince pies and cocoa. One house had a beautiful Christmas tree that was so tall it nearly reached the ceiling!

Fun fact
The biggest selling single of all time is *White Christmas* recorded by Bing Crosby in 1942. It has sold well over 30,000,000 copies.

In the evenings my family sang carols together at home, too. My mum played the piano and we all joined in. Sometimes my Auntie May brought her wind-up **gramophone** so we could listen to records together. I only had two records but I played them over and over again: one was called *White Christmas* and the other was called *Little Brown Jug*.

During the war, Christmas was still a happy time even though it was harder to celebrate. When I was five, Stoneleigh started to get bombed and I went to stay with my Auntie Nell in Truro, Cornwall. I didn't feel homesick because my mum and brother came, too. Most **evacuees** were not so lucky: they had to spend Christmas away from their homes and families.

Fun fact
The largest number of Christmas cards ever sent out by one person was 62, 824. They were sent out by Werner Erhard of San Fransico, USA in December 1975.

People collected presents and organised Christmas parties for the evacuees to help cheer them up.

The evacuees in this picture were given sweets and toys by American soldiers who came to Britain to work with the armed forces.

During air-raids people had to stay inside specially built shelters to keep safe from bombs. At Christmas time some people even had Christmas parties in their shelter! These people have decorated their shelter with paper chains and lanterns to make it look more cheerful.

My dad couldn't spend Christmas with us because he was a soldier in the army. Most other families had relatives away from home, too. We sent my dad a Christmas card and my mum wrote him a letter on an airgraph form, which was specially made to send to people in the armed forces.

SEND CHRISTMAS CARDS TO ALL AT HOME

GIVE WINGS TO YOUR THOUGHTS
SEND HIM A
CHRISTMAS CARD

Christmas Carols

Christmas was an exciting time at school because we put on a play for our mums and dads to come and watch. One year I was chosen to play one of the angels in the **nativity** play.

You could only be an angel if you went to ballet lessons because you had to dance on stage. My mum helped me make a costume out of an old sheet. Another year we put on a play called *The Two Books that Came Alive.* The photo on the left shows my class dressed up in our costumes.

We had fun in the classroom, too. Instead of having our usual lessons we made Christmas decorations to put up at home. Our teacher taught us how to make paper chains using paper stuck with glue and paper lanterns which we coloured with crayons.

Everyone in my class made a pop-up Christmas card to give to their mum and dad. This is how you make it.

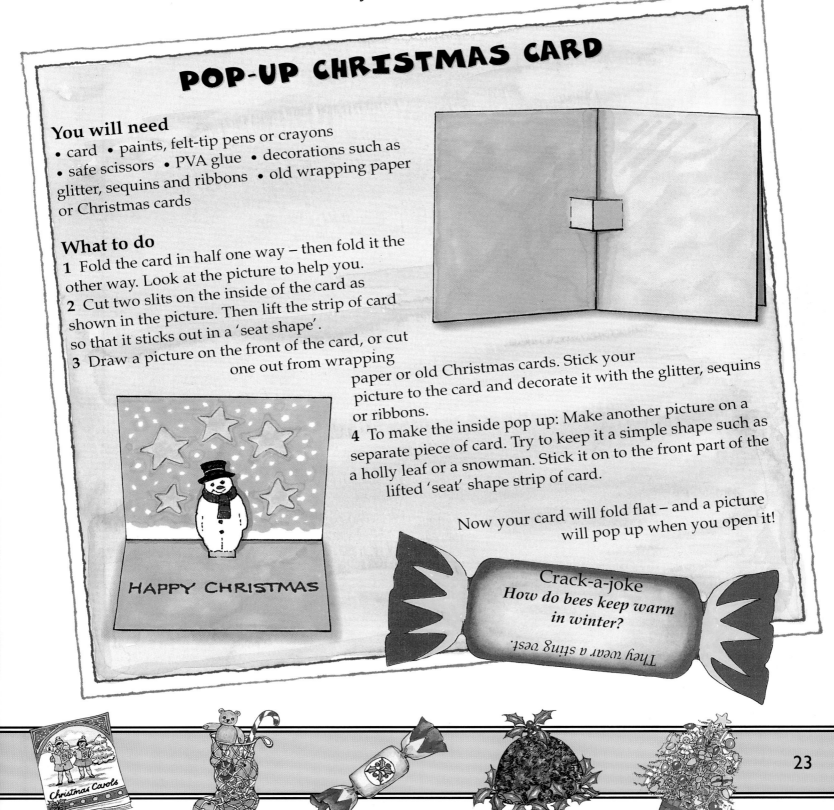

POP-UP CHRISTMAS CARD

You will need
- card • paints, felt-tip pens or crayons
- safe scissors • PVA glue • decorations such as glitter, sequins and ribbons • old wrapping paper or Christmas cards

What to do

1 Fold the card in half one way – then fold it the other way. Look at the picture to help you.

2 Cut two slits on the inside of the card as shown in the picture. Then lift the strip of card so that it sticks out in a 'seat shape'.

3 Draw a picture on the front of the card, or cut one out from wrapping paper or old Christmas cards. Stick your picture to the card and decorate it with the glitter, sequins or ribbons.

4 To make the inside pop up: Make another picture on a separate piece of card. Try to keep it a simple shape such as a holly leaf or a snowman. Stick it on to the front part of the lifted 'seat' shape strip of card.

Now your card will fold flat – and a picture will pop up when you open it!

HAPPY CHRISTMAS

Crack-a-joke
How do bees keep warm in winter?

They wear a sting vest.

We spent most of Christmas Eve decorating the house ready for Christmas Day. A lot of our decorations were home-made, but we had some we'd bought, too. All the decorations were kept in a cardboard box under the stairs. Some of the decorations were quite a few years old but we looked after them carefully so they could be used again.

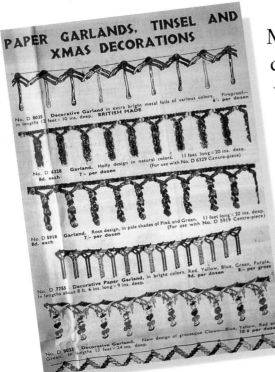

Most decorations were made out of coloured paper, not plastic like they are now. They unfolded to make pretty shapes that you hung on the walls or from the ceiling. The paper was very thin and fragile so you had to hold each decoration very gently.

We even had a
paper Christmas tree! It stored
flat and unfolded to make the shape
of a miniature fir tree when you
hung it up. It was green all over
except for the
bottom part
which was
bright red and
shaped like a bucket.

GLITTERING
Christmas
FROST

'My brother and I made some decorations.'

At my school all the children made paper lanterns like this one.

Fun fact
In the last ninety-seven years, London has only had eight 'snowing' or white Christmas Days.

☆ PAPER ☆ LANTERNS ☆

You will need
- strong coloured paper (15cm wide X 25cm long) • PVA glue
- safe scissors • paint, spray, glitter (anything you want to decorate your lantern) • a piece of string

What to do

1 Fold the paper in half lengthwise.

2 Fold up two narrow strips along each long edge.

3 Cut the paper into evenly spaced strips, up to the fold.

4 Open up the paper and glue the two ends together (so the folds are top and bottom).

5 Decorate your lantern with paint, glitter, or spray.

6 Fix a loop of string to the top of the lantern so you can hang it up.

My brother and I made some decorations at home, too. The decorations on this page are easy to make and can be as colourful as you like!

☆CRÊPE☆ ☆PAPER☆TWISTS☆

You will need
- 2 long strips of different coloured crêpe paper
- a stapler

What to do

1 Staple both strips of paper together at one end.

2 Wrap the red strip over the top of the blue strip.

3 Take the blue strip and wrap it over the top of the red strip.

4 Keep wrapping the strips over each other until all the paper has been used.

5 Staple the ends of the strips together.

6 Pull the twist open to decorate your walls.

☆SNOW☆FLAKES☆

You will need
- a fairly large square piece of white paper   • safe scissors
- small bits of foil, some glitter or spray to decorate the snowflake
- PVA glue for sticking glitter or foil   • a piece of string, sellotape or Blu-tack to fix the snowflake

What to do

1 Fold the paper across, then across again to make a smaller square.

2 Fold this diagonally, corner to corner to make a triangle.

3 Cut out shapes along two or all of the long edges, (make sure you don't cut to the very end of each edge or the snowflake will break).

4 Unfold the paper to show a snowflake.

5 Decorate the snowflake as you like.

6 Hang your snowflake from the ceiling with string or stick it to the inside of a window.

When I was eight and the war had ended, my dad bought our first Christmas tree. It was a little artificial one with silver tinsel branches like the tree in this photo. I liked it much more than the paper tree because we could hang decorations on it. My mum brought a set of coloured glass baubles to hang on the tree. They were very fragile and I wasn't allowed to touch them in case I broke them.

In those days people who had real Christmas trees often decorated them with lighted candles. We decorated our artificial tree with a string of tiny, coloured light bulbs. On top of the tree we put a beautiful wax fairy dressed in a white ballerina dress.

We listened to Christmas shows on the wireless while we decorated the tree.

MAZDA ELECTRIC Decoration LAMP OUTFIT

We also made silver bells to hang on our Christmas tree. This is how you make them.

☆ SILVER ☆ BELLS ☆

You will need
- a cardboard egg box • silver foil • safe scissors
- coloured string or tinsel

What to do

1 Cut out the 6 cups from the egg box.
2 Cover each egg cup with silver foil (don't forget to cover the insides, too!), moulding it to the bell-shape of the egg cup.
3 Turn each bell upside down and make a small hole through the top.
4 Divide the bells into pairs.
5 Thread a piece of string or tinsel through the hole in one bell and tie a large knot at one end, so the bell can't fall off.
6 Thread the other end of the string or tinsel through the hole in the second bell and tie a knot at the end to hold that bell secure.
7 Hang the bells on your Christmas tree. They also look pretty over the corners of picture frames or over paper chains.

Crack-a-joke
What animals fall from the clouds?
Rain-deer.

29

In the days before Christmas, Peter and I raced down the stairs every morning to see what the postman had brought.

We took it in turns to open the Christmas cards. During the war my dad sent us lots of letters, too. Sometimes the postman brought us a parcel, but Mum wouldn't let us open it until Christmas Day. We had some friends in Holland who always sent us a tin of iced biscuits and gingerbread. My cousins usually sent us a Christmas present each, too.

Fun fact
The first Christmas card was sent out in 1843 by Sir Henry Cole. People didn't start sending Christmas cards to each other regularly until 1862.

PLEASE ADDRESS YOUR REPLY TO

Rank CPL. No. 7954368.

Name EDWARDS R.W.

Address ADVANCE SQUADRON.
2ND ARMOURED REINFORCEMENT UNIT
% 2ND ARMOURED REINFORCEMENT GROUP
R.P.C. D.L.A.

Date 13/12/44

MY DARLING LITTLE LADY,
THIS LITTLE LETTER IS JUST
TO WISH YOU A VERY HAPPY CHRISTMAS
WITH LOTS OF FUN AND NICE THINGS
AND CREAM CAKES (!) TO EAT — BUT
DON'T TURN INTO A LITTLE — WILL
YOU! I SHALL BE THINKING OF
YOU ALL EVER SUCH A LOT — ALL
DAY CHRISTMAS DAY. GOOD NIGHT
MY DARLING GIRLIE, GOD BLESS YOU
AND KEEP YOU SAFE AND HAPPY
ALWAYS. WITH LOTS OF LOVE AND
STOCKINGS FULL OF KISSES FROM YOUR
EVER LOVING.
DADDY.

XXXXXXXX

NATIONAL WAR EFFORT. PLEASE USE BOTH SIDES OF PAPER

Christmas was a busy time for my mum in the kitchen. Most people made their own Christmas puddings and Christmas cakes. Ready-made Christmas puddings like the one in this photo were expensive and few families could afford to buy them.

Everyone in my family took it in turns to stir the Christmas pudding mixture and make a wish.

CWS CHRISTMAS PUDDING
BOIL FOR 2 HOURS
CO-OPERATIVE WHOLESALE SOC. LTD.
1, BALLOON STREET, MANCHESTER.
PRESERVE WORKS:
NET WEIGHT · DDLETON, READING, · TON, STOCKTON, ARNSLEY, WISBECH.
2 lb.

Afterwards, my mum put some silver threepenny pieces into the mixture; enough for one coin each.

What is Christmas without mince-pies?
What are mince-pies without

Mc Dougall's
SELF-RAISING FLOUR

Mum steamed the pudding in the copper boiler that heated our water for washing. It made the kitchen very hot and steamy!

When I was little, there was a shortage of sweets and people weren't able to buy as many Christmas goodies as usual. We had to make our own sweets instead!

Here are some of the recipes I used to make with my mum. Now you can try them, too!

PEPPERMINT STARS

You will need
- 500g icing sugar
- 1 teaspoon peppermint essence
- 1 dessertspoon cream
- 1 cardboard star (you can trace the star shape on this page to make your own)
- 1 egg white
- edible silver balls

What to do
1 Sieve the icing sugar to get rid of any lumps.
2 Whisk the egg white until it turns fluffy.
3 Mix together the icing sugar, cream and peppermint.
4 Add enough of the egg white to make a stiff paste.
5 Put the paste on to a wooden board (sprinkle some icing sugar on the board first, to stop the paste from sticking).
6 Use your fingers to knead the paste for five minutes.
7 Leave the paste for one hour.
8 Roll out the paste until it's about 15mm thick.
9 Put the cardboard star on top of the paste and use a knife to cut around the shape carefully.
10 Decorate the stars with silver balls.
11 Leave to set for a few hours before eating.

Christmas Carols

COCONUT ICE

You will need
- 500g icing sugar
- 100g desiccated coconut
- 1 tablespoon milk
- 1 egg white
- pink food colouring
- greaseproof paper

What to do
1 Sieve the icing sugar to get rid of any lumps.
2 Add the coconut and milk and stir well.
3 Whisk the egg white until it's fluffy.
4 Add some of the egg white to the mixture to make it into a soft paste.
5 Cover the bottom of the tin with a piece of greaseproof paper.
6 Put half of the paste into the tin.
7 Add a few drops of food colouring to the rest of the paste and knead with your fingers until it's pink.
9 Put the pink paste on top of the white paste and press both together.
10 Leave to set.

MINI CHRISTMAS LOGS

You will need
- 250g marzipan
- 50g chocolate powder
- 1 egg white

What to do
1 Cut the marzipan into small pieces.
2 Use your fingers to shape the marzipan into little logs.
3 Make a pattern on top of the logs using a fork.
4 Brush the logs with egg white.
5 Roll the logs in chocolate powder until they are brown all over.
6 Leave to dry before eating.

Fun fact
The world's biggest mince pie was 6m wide and 1.5m tall. It weighed over one tonne and was baked at Ashby-de-la-Zouch, Leicestershire in 1932.

Before we went to bed on Christmas Eve, my brother and I wrote a letter to Santa, telling him what we wanted for Christmas. I wanted to keep my wish secret, so I put my arms around my letter to stop Peter seeing what I was writing. We posted our letters up the chimney above the fire in our living room.

GREETINGS ★ 1943

The draught from the fire carried our letters up the chimney. Sometimes we wrote two or three letters each, just in case the first one didn't reach Santa.

34

We went to bed early but I was too excited to fall asleep straight away. I spent a long time looking out of the window, trying to see Santa Claus. At about half-past ten, Mum woke us up to walk to midnight mass in the local church. I put on my best coat and a pair of woolly mittens because it was cold inside the church. At Christmas time the church was filled with special decorations. I liked to see the nativity scene.

It was made of little wooden figures and straw and was lit up by candles. At the front of the church there was a huge Christmas tree. We all sang carols and the choir boys carried lanterns in a long procession.

Crack-a-joke
Why did King Arthur buy long woollen underwear?
For the cold winter knights.

After midnight mass we rushed home to put out our stockings for Santa. The stockings were made out of net, specially for Christmas. They were about 50cm long and about 10cm wide, so only small presents would fit inside. I put my stocking on the bottom of my bed.

As soon as I woke up on Christmas morning I wiggled my toes to see if I could feel the weight of the stocking on my feet. If it felt heavy I knew that Santa had been.

Peter and I raced to open our presents. Each gift was wrapped in brown paper and tied with string so opening them was quite a noisy job! We took our presents into Mum and Dad's bedroom to show them what Santa had brought us.

Crack-a-joke
What do you get if you cross an icicle with a fierce dog?

Frost bite.

At the bottom of the stocking there was always an orange or an apple, some chocolate money and a shiny new penny. Then we had one or two small gifts like a box of pencils, a colouring book, a bag of sweets or a little toy. My mum and dad gave us one present each, too. One year I got a doll dressed in a flying suit and my brother got a set of lead soldiers.

Sometimes we were given annuals like the *Radio Fun Annual* or a *Rupert Annual*.

One year Peter got a model building kit and I got a set of sewing cards called 'Stitchem': you sewed around the drawing on each card to make a picture.

On Christmas morning Dad lit the fire in the living room earlier than usual and piled it extra high with coal. We ate a cooked breakfast of poached eggs and **black pudding**. After breakfast Peter and I played with our new toys and my mum started cooking the Christmas dinner.

My grandad, Auntie May, Auntie Trixie and Uncle Harry came to our house for Christmas dinner. During the war we used our **Morrison shelter** as a dinner table. It was made of strong steel and had wire mesh sides. The sharp corners often bruised my legs so I didn't like it much!

Fun fact
In 1943 each butcher with 800 registered customers was rationed to just 15 turkeys.

We ate chicken for Christmas dinner. When I was little, chicken was quite expensive and Christmas was the only time we ate it! Most families grew their own vegetables. We ate potatoes and Brussels sprouts from our garden.

Crack-a-joke

What do monkeys sing at Christmas?

Jungle bells.

The arrival of the Christmas pudding was quite an event! My dad carried it from the kitchen to the table and we made a noisy procession behind him. Peter banged two saucepan lids together and I played a tune on a comb and a piece of tissue paper.

When everyone was seated at the table again, we pulled our crackers and put on paper hats. Then we took it in turns to read aloud the jokes found inside each cracker. Here are some of my favourite cracker jokes.

Fun fact

The first Christmas cracker was made in 1846. The world's biggest Christmas cracker was nearly 46m long and over 3m wide. It was pulled in a car park in Sydney, Australia on 9 November 1991.

Crack-a-joke

What lives at the South Pole and smiles?

A pen-grin.

Crack-a-joke

What do you call a deer that can see well?

A good eye-deer.

My grandad and my aunties brought us Christmas presents but we didn't open them until the afternoon. My mum hid them upstairs with the parcels that had arrived in the post. After dinner my brother dressed up as Santa Claus to carry the presents downstairs. He wore a pair of wellies, my mum's red dressing-gown, a red hat and a cotton-wool beard and carried the parcels in an old pillow case.

Fun fact
The first Royal Christmas message was broadcast on the radio by King George V in 1932.

When all the presents had been opened, the grown-ups listened to the King's speech on the wireless and we played with our toys. At the end of the King's speech, everyone stood up while the national anthem was played.

Crack-a-joke
What card game do crocodiles play?

Snap.

Afterwards we played card games like happy families and snap and board games like Monopoly and snakes and ladders.

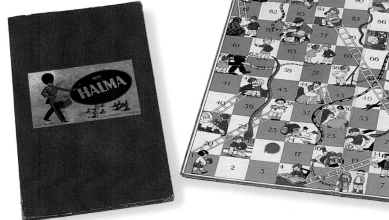

My grandad liked to play a game called halma. It was a bit like draughts but you played it using wooden pegs.

We didn't have a television to watch or computer games to play with, so we had to make our own fun. One year my uncle put on a puppet show using a miniature cardboard theatre and Auntie May's gramophone for music.

'I went to bed feeling very full.'

One of our favourite games was called consequences. It's a good game to play after Christmas dinner because you don't have to move about very much!

CONSEQUENCES

How to play

Everyone needs to have a long, thin piece of paper and a pencil. One person is the 'caller' and has to call out a set of instructions to the others. For example the caller will ask each person to write down a boy's name. Each person writes down their answer and then folds back that part of the paper so no-one else can read it. Then he/she passes their piece of paper to the person sitting on their right.

The person who receives the paper writes down the next part of the story that the caller calls out. Then they fold the paper and pass it to the person on their right. And so on. At the end of the game, everyone reads out what is written on the piece of paper they are holding. You should end up with some very funny stories!

Here is a sequence to help you: 1) boy's name 2) girl's name 3) place where they met 4) the day that they met 5) the time that they met 6) what he said to her 7) what she said to him 8) what was the result (the consequence).

You could also play this game by drawing a sequence of different body parts to make a funny picture of a person instead.

Crack-a-joke
What has feathers and rides a broomstick to the beach?

A turkey sand-witch.

Crack-a-joke
What do you get if you cross a whale with a cabbage?

Brussels spouts.

We had a big Christmas tea together at about six o'clock. There were plates of bread and butter with home-made jam, mincepies and Christmas cake. Every year my mum made a family recipe called Edward's Special. It was a sort of chocolate trifle with coconut sprinkled on the top. I always went to bed feeling very full on Christmas Day!

Christmas was very exciting when I was young. We didn't have as much as people do now, but it was a special time for everyone. We had happy times then.

Loving Christmas Greetings

The Armed Forces The army, navy and airforce.

Latin An ancient Roman language sometimes used in church services and singing.

Gramophone A record player.

Evacuees People who moved from a city made dangerous by bombing to a safer place in the countryside.

Nativity The birth of Jesus.

Black pudding A kind of sausage.

Morrison shelter A metal frame that people hid under during air-raids to keep safe from bombs.

OTHER BOOKS TO READ

Other books about twentieth-century history for younger readers published by Evans include:

Rainbows *When Grandma Was Young*
Rainbows *When Dad Was Young*
Rainbows *What Was It Like Before Television?*
Tell Me About *Emmeline Pankhurst*
Tell Me About *Enid Blyton*

Britain Through The Ages *Britain Since 1930*
Alpha *1960s*
Take Ten Years *1930s, 1940s, 1950s, 1960s, 1970s, 1980s*

INDEX

O. R.